Quiet Disruptors

QUIET
DISRUPTORS

Creating Change Without Shouting

SUE HEATHERINGTON

Published by:
Waterside Voices,
 (*part of The Waterside (Swansea) Ltd*)
Ty Blaenant Ddu,
Felindre, Swansea,
SA5 7ND UK

watersidevoices.com

Typesetting: Steve Heatherington

Cover Design: Katia Lord, Design Mind Studio

Cover photo: Sue Heatherington

ISBN-13: 979 8 59151 440 2

+2

Dedicated to

Steve, my friend for life.

Contents

Welcome

'Hello, I'm Sue Heatherington, and I'm a quiet disruptor.'

Nothing prepared me for the extraordinary response when I started using this introduction in the Summer of 2018.

Yes, there was a momentary pause as this apparently contradictory phrase landed. But instead of questioning it, some immediately picked it up and started trying it on for size.

It was as if I had offered them a beautifully wrapped gift, and they were eager to unwrap it. What they found inside has started to revolutionise lives. Not overnight, but an exploration of what it could mean to be a different kind of change-maker.

So where did this phrase come from?

I needed a simple way to make sense of my untypical life that conveyed enough, without being overwhelming. We had just gone through several challenging years, including family trauma, business chaos and serious illnesses. And my CV included big jobs and pioneering work across a wide range of sectors.

Recovering from surgery for breast cancer gave me time to reflect on where we were and reconnect with writers and activists I admired. The enforced rest also started revealing the years of rubbish I'd allowed others to put on me, and how I'd become isolated, worn out and diminished.

I realised that we could make a difference without shouting. And there is a place for thoughtful and creative change-makers, who don't conform to the familiar model of superhero.

However, I knew I couldn't do this solo. I was spent and battered. Therefore, I jumped at the opportunity of joining Bernadette Jiwa's *the* Right Company—a global business community of like-minded people.

But how to introduce myself to these lovely people?

'quiet disruptor'

It was just a phrase, but it ignited something, giving hope and permission to explore a different way to make a difference.

Finding the others, in *the* Right Company and elsewhere, was a revelation. These were not noisy, aggressive or reactive people, and their generous and gentle footprints were in every area of work and life.

But there was nothing passive about how they were changing the conversation around them. This wasn't a kind of benign fatalism. Neither was it safe. My years of prodding traditional approaches to farming, leadership and healthcare had already taught me that!

Instead, this shift in the narrative required a level of honesty and courage. Firstly, with ourselves about what we really care about and how far we are willing to step out. And then how we learn to use our voice and be ourselves, rather than borrow from someone else.

However, I realised that this was also a reflection of a wider cultural shift. Collectively we are in the middle of a major transition in history and this is becoming evident in all areas of our lives. There is a sense that these emerging quiet disruptors are ripe for such a time as this.

So it's just the start of the journey.

Navigating the book

This is more of a guidebook than a textbook. Designed to inspire, encourage and provoke, I hope you'll find space to pause and reflect. It's not a race to the end!

Part 1: Why Now?

> 'For last year's words belong to last year's language and next year's words await another voice.'
>
> TS ELIOT, FROM LITTLE GIDDING, FOUR QUARTETS

We need a new language for a new era. One fit to handle the different landscape we are now entering, because this is no longer the industrial age, with its assumptions of clear boundaries and simple, linear answers.

These introductory chapters map the shifts we are going through, and why we are seeing a different kind of change.

The Manifesto for Quiet Disruptors gives voice to these new change-makers and in seeing them more clearly, we understand why they are becoming more evident at this time.

Part 2: New Voices of Curiosity, Creativity and Connection

This is a different kind of change, and we need to tune into different voices.

Through the stories of people who could be described as quiet disruptors we see the emerging importance of having fresh eyes, new creative expressions and the shift in culture that will enable us all to flourish in this new age.

And here's the thing. They aren't all alike. The contributions they are making express their individual DNA. Their voice is distinctive, even though they may have common drivers.

Part 3: Change the Conversation

So what are we going to do with this?

This immensely practical part of the book offers the foundations for becoming the change we want to see, with suggestions on how to find:

- your friends
- your voice
- your space

And then step across the threshold.

Resources

All good guidebooks offer resources for readers to do their own exploration.

Here you'll find all of the people mentioned in the book, along with a brief introduction, relevant material and links for each of them.

And there are also further Quiet Disruptor resources available on the website and elsewhere.

And as we start...

Pause,
see with fresh eyes,
understand where
you are.

Put on
your own name
and cross this
threshold.

For this
time is now
waiting for
you.

Sue Heatherington
South West Wales
December 2020

PART 1: WHY NOW?

1

A timely paradox

'When you have something to say you don't need to shout'

Isn't it extraordinary?

We live in a world that is always on and often noisy. And those who speak loudest and speak first seem to have the dominance. They are the ones all over the media, and we struggle to turn the volume down.

But are there other voices?

There have always been quiet disruptors. Thoughtful and creative change-makers, who are driven by something bigger than themselves, who look to the horizon. People like Galileo, Marie Curie, Gandhi and Rosa Parks. They were not always seen or understood, and were often treated as an irritant or irrelevance.

Today, we might say that we need an antidote to the current culture, we are rebalancing the scales. However, I suspect there is more going on.

Lifting the lid

Our culture—our way of thinking about and being in the world—has been primarily shaped by the industrial age.

We recognise the structure and process, and assume that if you do X, then Y will happen. It's relatively binary, and there are few grey areas.

However, when something emerges that is both/and it doesn't easily fit. It feels uncomfortable and gets pushed to the margins. 'Let's close the lid...'

To many of us it is clear that the industrial age is coming to an inglorious close. It is broken, and the cracks are increasingly evident. Our superheroes are fallible humans like the rest of us and hierarchies are crumbling. But this isn't just demise; it's also the birth of the new. We just don't know what to call it, yet.

We see evidence of this emergence in a greater awareness of the complexity and interconnectedness in the world. The internet makes us a global village, and we can communicate with people we will never meet. And we don't need others to give us permission.

We also see it in the rise of unpredictability and chaos. We have more data but fewer answers. Our illusion of control is evaporating. We realise that we cannot determine our future.

This has been brought home most recently by the pandemic. No one has been untouched by this. And no one has a solution to all the challenges, at least not at the time of writing.

We're revisiting the things we thought were absolute and realising that maybe we need a different set of lenses to understand where we are and navigate forward.

In this emerging landscape more of us are becoming open to the both/and rather than relying on either/or. Paradox and polarities have a place and provide a way to grow that transcends linear or fixed mindsets.

This is showing up in a variety of unexpected places. Not least in how we think about people and understand change.

People across all generations, especially Millennials and GenZ, are asking fundamental questions about meaning. Including about our responsibility to the planet and our fellow human beings.

This is starting to shift our relationships, our connection to material possessions and time, and our sense of who we are and why we are here.

And it is challenging the way we organise our work and our world.

A new paradox

In this context, the language of 'quiet' has a place.

Susan Cain's *Quiet Revolution*—TED Talk, books and movement—has done a brilliant job of giving permission and vocabulary to those of us who may be more reflective. Not necessarily introvert or antisocial but tending to be more in our heads. We probably need more space and quiet than others to do our best work and flourish.

But for quiet disruptors, encouragement to be comfortable and secure in our own world isn't enough. The things that we care about motivate us to seek change and do things differently. To paraphrase Tony Campolo in *Carpe Diem*, we don't want to tiptoe through life just to arrive at death safely.

Therefore, standing by and letting the status quo continue isn't ok. We have to do something about it. But we want to do it in a way that resonates with who we are, not borrow someone else's clothes or megaphone.

Hence the paradox: being quiet and disruptive. It's already happening.

The power to change

Here's the thing: only people make change.

Arguably, nothing changes without the initiation of a human being, somewhere. But the tools we use can alter everything, faster than we realise.

We are currently seeing the biggest shift in history for centuries, yet we are mostly oblivious to its enormity. Being connected and having access to information through the internet is so much part of our lives, it's hard to remember life before.

And the next iteration, could be even more significant.

For people who want to make change happen, this level of connection ultimately moves the goalposts. Previously it was largely dependent on power. Did you have enough money or resources? Were you in a senior enough role? Did you have a significant enough voice, or were you given permission?

No more.

If you have something to say, you can say it. If you want to influence others, there are groups you can connect with. You don't need to be buried in a job for life in a traditional organisation, because their roles are becoming obsolete in the new world.

But also, the speed at which data and knowledge are increasing is exponential. There is no way that any individual can keep up. Therefore, being a traditional expert or having technical authority is increasingly short-lived.

It's about a different set of skills and orientation, not ones you learn to pass the test. Being able to make meaning, see patterns, understand people and create connections. Going deeper, not to discover 'the right answer' but to interpret complexity in an unpredictable, yet increasingly relational world.

In 1934 T S Eliot wrote *Choruses from The Rock*, in which he captured this astonishing insight:

> Where is the Life we have lost in living?
>
> Where is the wisdom we have lost in
>   knowledge?
>
> Where is the knowledge we have lost in
>   information?
>
> *TS ELIOT*

And it's not a minute out of date!

More than ever, we are in a relational world where titles and hierarchies matter less than trust, connection and purpose. Our degrees of separation to every other inhabitant of the planet is reducing rapidly. And people care much more about belonging.

This means that we can do more with less if we find a way to make connections.

2

The Manifesto for Quiet Disruptors

Because it's time to change the conversation for good.

Have you noticed? We're shifting from one era to the next.

From the modern, industrial age with linear and predictable answers, to a complex, interconnected and volatile world. Where what we do affects who others become and impacts our whole environment, without us fully realising it.

We need different voices—people with fresh things to say who don't need to shout.

Not just super-heroes with confident gestures. Nor the loud, always-on culture, with quick answers that offer attractive sticking plasters, yet fail to see what comes next or why we are doing it anyway.

But the thoughtful and creative change-makers who look from the edge and craft their responses, who want to make a difference, differently. Not just for today.

Because more of the same won't do.

So now is our time to shift the conversation by becoming the change we want to see. Owning our voice, finding the others and having the courage to speak softly about things that matter.

Because only people make change. And change emerges with those who have the courage to be different:

- *who think before they speak;*

- *who ask questions we'd sometimes rather not face;*

- *who create solutions we hadn't expected;*

- *who see more from the edge, than the centre, and make connections that surprise us;*

- *who are driven to make a difference, but want to do it differently, with grace;*

- *who get their energy from calm reflection, beautiful ideas, and taking the long view;*

- *who exercise kindness, generosity and stubborn courage in pursuing a different way of looking, being and doing that can turn our world upside down—for the better.*

It's time for the new change-makers.

The quiet disruptors with the courage to speak softly about things that matter.

3

Meet the new change-makers

'I've learned that people will forget what you said, people will forget what you did, but people will never forget how you made them feel.'

MAYA ANGELOU IN CONVERSATION WITH BRENÈ BROWN

in 2008 David and Clare Hieatt did something extraordinary.

They gathered a bunch of people in a field over a few days and started to explore how to create a safe space to ask better questions. The Do Lectures—the encouragement network—was born.

Now running distinctive events, including online, and spawning a small library of Do Books because 'ideas change things', the impact of what happens when you bring passionate, thoughtful and creative people together is felt globally. People are discovering and reaching for their potential. New businesses, social enterprise, creative movements and much more have grown as a result of what started in a cowshed.

And that's not all. David and Clare also stepped into new territory to restore jean-making to their small town in far West Wales, because it mattered.

But none of this has been done conventionally. Indeed, The Hiut Denim Company doesn't sell jeans, so much as offer access to a tribe whose members include well-known creatives, musicians and entrepreneurs across the world.

And of course, the jeans are fab and ethically sound.

An emerging story

It isn't what people know, or how powerful they are, but who they enable us to become that matters now.

We are slowly shifting from meaning based on material possessions and traditional status, to something altogether different. Not that this is universal, and some might argue that this is the privilege of the West speaking. But there are echoes all around.

David and Clare Hieatt, and the team are evidence of an emerging story about doing change differently. The Do Lectures have impacted many people directly and indirectly in the last ten years. And of the 400 people who used to make jeans in Cardigan, a number now have their jobs back.

I also think about Seth Godin, writer, speaker and entrepreneur with wise things to say about marketing, business, learning and culture. He doesn't shout on social media, yet his thoughtful and provocative daily blog—which he's been writing consistently since 2004—now has over 700,000 subscribers. He is clear on what he stands for and has intentionally developed his voice. As a result, there are thousands of people across the world 'making a ruckus' in a way they probably wouldn't have had the courage, tenacity or insight to do previously.

And then there are the clinicians who are calling time on the traditional doctor: patient relationship and the way healthcare is often delivered. Their 'enough is enough' includes experimenting with who sits in the 'big chair' in the consulting room. Upsetting the usual power dynamics in medicine with astonishing results.

Or the myriad of people who have left traditional jobs to set up their own businesses or social enterprise. They recognise that the idea of a 'job for life' is no longer feasible or even desirable, and want to make an impact through their work.

There are the artists, activists like the anonymous Banksy, who are using their voice to draw attention to things we'd rather not see. Or new writers who no longer need the patronage of big publishing houses to be read.

These are just examples of what has emerged in the last decade, with roots that often go further back. The internet has profoundly affected their ability to see and be seen, to create generous space and offer their voice to anyone who has ears to hear.

There are many more to come. And as we start to adjust our way of seeing and listening, we will discover them. Sometimes emerging from the most unlikely places.

So who are the quiet disruptors?

That's a profoundly simple question with two easy answers: those who think they are; and those who look like they might be.

Of course, easy answers often come with hidden depths.

So if you were looking for a tidy description of 'type', then I'm sorry. There is no box. And that's the whole point. We are no longer in a linear world where everything has hard edges.

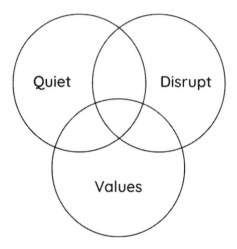

However, we can trace the core elements of being quiet, being disruptive and being driven by values as threads that are emerging more widely in our current era. And they come together now in a unique blend in quiet disruptors, who are becoming more visible.

- **QUIET** Susan Cain was not the first person to talk about introversion, but her *Quiet: The Power of Introverts in a World that Can't Stop Talking* has spawned a revolution. People who didn't want to be defined by the dominant culture finally had a language to talk about who they were. And others started to recognise it too.

- **DISRUPTIVE** While Clayton Christensen was one of the first to name the importance of disruption in innovation in 1997, he certainly wasn't the last. Given the subsequent global events many more are challenging the way we do things. Disruption—whether as pirates, rebels, radical change-makers, originals or simply questioning why we do things because they don't seem to be working that well—is current. And the voices are getting more insistent.

- **VALUES** At the same time, people are also digging deeper into the values and choices that have shaped their lives. Again, clear voices are offering an alternative if we will stop and look at ourselves. Greg McKeown's challenge of less but better in *Essentialism: The Disciplined Pursuit of Less* typifies this thread. And many have embraced minimalism in its various forms. People and companies are taking time to strengthen their values in this turbulent sea, knowing that they both anchor them and shape their story, enabling them to be seen.

These movements are positive and provide inspiration and resources for quiet disruptors. But they are not sufficient.

Not all quiet disruptors want to be labelled as introverts, and they don't want to remain comfortable and secure in a corner. What drives them—their values, convictions and principles—pushes them out into uncomfortable territory to create the change they want to see.

But neither do they want the megaphones of traditional dissidents. They want to explore an alternative way of making their voice heard, one that doesn't violate the kind of person they want to be.

And the values that drive them only have meaning and expression in the context of a bigger story. This isn't just about them, and an insular way of being in the world, even though it may resemble the tenacious focus that others bring.

Each person who identifies as being a quiet disruptor will have their individual, unique fingerprint. No one is the same, though in my experience they often discover a resonance. And what they do—how and where they make that identity visible—could look very different. However, the generic fruit might be remarkably similar.

You might find them in a wide variety of places, both inside organisations and running their own show. However, there may be locations where they are more likely to be found.

For example, I wonder if proportionately there are more outside of the mainstream, as this will allow more self-determination and more nuanced expression. Quiet disruptors usually don't rely on someone else to tell them what to do.

Conversely, they are probably less well represented at senior levels within hierarchical and bureaucratic organisations. They may be less willing to play power games and may not be promoted in a culture dominated by those who speak first and think later.

They are probably more evident in grassroots community activism as they inspire confidence by their creative thinking and commitment to the cause. Just don't ask them to be constantly loud, or always on.

And of course, there are plenty of people who have found their creative voice as writers, artists, designers and musicians, and have something to say.

So this isn't a label or a badge, but potentially a powerful way of seeing a new kind of thoughtful and creative change-maker. Those who will help us navigate our emerging world in a better way.

Reframing change

This is because the kind of change we need has fundamentally altered, and this impacts us all.

And this is where the potential contribution of people who are quiet disruptors comes into its own, positively. We need their curiosity, their creativity and their convictions if we are to navigate forward well. And in the process, they will help reshape our culture, the way we do things together that will benefit everyone.

So, it's time for the new change-makers. *'...who exercise kindness, generosity and stubborn courage in pursuing a different way of looking, being and doing that can turn our world upside down—for the better.'*

Just don't expect them to turn up in superhero outfits or shout in the streets.

PART 2: NEW VOICES OF CURIOSITY, CREATIVITY AND CONNECTION

FRESH EYES

'The real voyage of discovery consists not in finding new landscapes but in seeing with new eyes'

MARCEL PROUST

4

The case for curiosity

'Once recognised, the quiet yet persistent voice of curi-
osity doesn't go away'

SETH GODIN IN TRIBES

If you listen to Simon Sinek in conversation, you realise he's an unshakable optimist and an unintentional
superstar. Nearly 50 million people have seen his 2009
TED talk and his first book *Start With Why* has radically
affected leaders and organisations across the globe. And
he's genuinely surprised.

He's always been curious, interested in trying things
out, understanding why people do the things they do.
Quickly realising that a career in law wasn't a good fit,
he moved into marketing and advertising.

Noticing that the same kind of spend on marketing ap-
peared to have different outcomes for different companies,
he wondered why. Being the thoughtfully persistent, kind
of person he is, this had to be pursued. And pursued. What
were the successful companies doing, especially as their
products weren't always that remarkable?

It was the second thread of curiosity about the biology of
the brain that led Simon to make sense of what he was
seeing. His Golden Circle—painted like a target with *why*

in the middle, followed by *how* and *what*—potentially upended the traditional way of thinking about business and marketing.

Perhaps it wasn't about *what* companies do, nor their particular approach to *how* they do it (their unique selling point), but *why* they do what they do that was the differentiator. And this was the issue: very few knew why. Indeed, only a minority even realised it was a question worth asking.

But it took the third step of curiosity to test this out. Would this approach work across the board, in different kinds of organisations? Does everyone have to start with why if they are to be successful?

In 2006 Simon closed his marketing strategy business and took the idea on the road, working with anyone who would listen and testing the concept to destruction. But it didn't fail. Instead, it has inspired thousands of organisations and millions of people across the world to uncover their why and discover their best way of working.

'Let us all choose to be the leaders we wish we had.'
SIMON SINEK

It all starts with curiosity

All of the discoveries and inventions we now take for granted started with curiosity. Someone, somewhere was exploring, wondering, questioning and not taking the existing answer as a given.

Now, we are awash with knowledge and information. However, we're starting to realise that while big data helps us understand how we got here, it can't imagine new ideas or create the 'not yet'.

Curiosity is becoming mainstream as Professor Francesca Gino persuasively argues in her 2018 Harvard Business Review article *The Business Case for Curiosity*. Her research shows that it leads to higher performing, more adaptable firms. And she is not alone.

So, where does curiosity come from? Or perhaps we should be asking why do we lose our natural childhood curiosity? As anyone who spends time around young children will know—they are not short on questions.

Children use their wondering, exploring and questioning to make sense of a world that they are encountering for the first time. In their case 'why?' is neither a factual nor a philosophical question, which is the reason our replies often completely fail to hit the mark.

However, it takes time and energy to stay with their curiosity, and our educational system does a poor job of that. Children quickly perceive that having the right answer is valued more highly than curiosity and great questions.

Over time we lose our curiosity muscles and our confidence to look at the world differently.

Rewards are given to those who are 'right', and our workplaces often complete the makeover, with bureaucratic processes designed to ensure compliance and standardisation. This is what league tables are based on, and the incentive to not question is high.

Against this backdrop, why are quiet disruptors more likely to have a higher curiosity quotient than many?

I think it is because being quiet, disruptive and value-driven leads to three interconnected characteristics:

- Deeper and broader thinking—because quiet disruptors tend to stand back to observe and reflect, they probe further and tend to ask more questions. You would not characterise them as short-term, reactive or superficial.

- Forward-looking—they are less likely to be defending an existing way of doing or seeing things. They are more ready to thoughtfully recognise failings and shortcomings and have the courage to do something about it.

- Passion driven—they might not be ultra-expressive, but they care deeply and have an underlying drive to see improvements in things they are concerned about. They won't lightly accept the status quo if it could be better.

What might this look like in everyday life? Where are their fresh eyes?

5

Questions are a gift

As a doctor, Atul Gawande was trained to understand how the human body works and recognise what it looks like when it's not functioning well.

As a surgeon, he was trained to operate to save lives and prevent harm.

As a writer with a background in philosophy and politics, he developed the skill of asking questions.

And this only scratches the surface of his activities, which also includes working with the World Health Organisation and leading public health non-profit organisations across the globe.

The thread that runs through much of his work is the intersection of failure and suffering. Why do people, especially clinicians, choose not to do something that could have led to a better outcome for their patients?

This is a profound question and one that walks into challenging territory.

When he started to investigate why the outcomes for surgery were so varied, it touched a sore point: that of medical culture and the inability to challenge doctors. Not only were death rates variable, but also how long it took for the evidence of good practice to be adopted universally. In some cases, this was up to 17 years.

'Why?' does not have a simple answer. But the solution of putting in place a simple surgical checklist that covers all the essential questions necessary to ensure effective intervention and good teamwork is a start. But that didn't make it easy!

This checklist has reduced deaths in surgery by up to 45%. And it started with curiosity and asking questions.

Questions are powerful, but not all questions are equal

The World Wide Web is the repository of more answers then we can begin to imagine. However, our capacity to frame good questions is becoming dulled by the 'helpfulness' of search engines.

Just start to type, or use voice activation, and our requirements are immediately anticipated. We're not used to waiting, and we've become lazy.

Powerful questions take time to frame and often require several iterations before use.

These aren't the simple 'yes or no' type of question, but those that take us deeper or broader. These are questions whose answers lead us to breakthrough insights, or strip away non-essential details so that the conclusions are laid bare. And demand a response.

Einstein is reported to have said that if he only had an hour to solve a problem on which his life depended; he would take 55 minutes to frame the question. Why? Because in the process, the answer would become evident.

Simon Sinek's work suggests there might be a hierarchy of questions, and Warren Berger's book *A More Beautiful Question* confirms it.

Warren is a journalist by training and was curious about the quality of answers in his profession, tracing back to the kind of questions asked. He concludes that the high-ranking questions are:

- Why?
- What if...?
- How?

All three, and especially the first two, connect with drivers of intent. We ask these questions when the answers are important to us at a level beyond knowing facts.

They also act as a multiplier. When we have asked the question at one level, our curiosity leads us further and unlocks even more questions. For example, going deeper with successive why's until we find the core issue.

The broadcaster and writer Krista Tippett never ceases to inspire me with her thoughtful and beautifully crafted questions shaped by her deep curiosity. The On Being Project includes an extraordinarily profound podcast, powerfully impacting both listeners and interviewees.

Better questions

So why might quiet disruptors be more likely to ask better questions?

Firstly, because they tend to be more thoughtful than reactive, they are likely to play with different questions in their heads to find the best fit before asking.

This means they are likely to be more intentional and deliberate in their thinking. Therefore, don't expect them to come up with their best offering with no preparation.

However, it is also because quiet disruptors are driven by their core values to change whatever they think is wrong. This feeds their courage to overcome the cultural bias of not challenging the status quo.

To ask questions is to disrupt because implicitly it says that things could be better. And that can feel messy and uncomfortable.

Often our culture is stacked against this kind of exchange. Not only do we rarely give time to frame questions well, but we also don't realise their value. We penalise those who ask, labelling them as troublemakers or time wasters.

But the consequences of assuming that easy answers serve us well is already becoming problematic with our political, social and organisational landscape littered with the results of short-term thinking.

I wonder, when was the last time someone asked a really good question in your organisation or team?

6

Seeing differently

'I've been looking differently at our world for some time now. It can feel like these are 'interesting times...' How do we imagine new futures, find wisdom and voice, and bring new meaning to life and work?'

DR STEVE MARSHALL

These lovely words of invitation usher us into the way that Steve Marshall sees the world.

Shaped by his eyes as a professional photographer, elite fighter pilot with acute attention to his situational awareness, and latterly as a consultant in organisational change and executive development, Steve now offers us a challenge.

Will we embrace the opportunity of #SeeingDifferently?

Steve's emerging Manifesto is a courageous step in reframing what we think we see that has vital implications. Even though he isn't shouting, people are listening for wisdom fit for our time.

Seeing more

'Our task is to read the things that are not yet on the page'

STEVE JOBS

Observing people who could be called quiet disruptors, the quality of responses they offer is often noticeable.

While they do not have a monopoly on great answers, there are emerging characteristics that often make them worth listening to:

- Broader perception—they appear to see and hear more

- Powerful insights—they often make extraordinary connections, including significant leaps

- Greater sensemaking—they are comfortable interpreting complexity and ambiguity (which we will explore in the next chapter)

Broader perception

Generally, the closer we are, the less we see, not of the detail, but the context. And often this is where significant insights lie.

In the 1980s, IBM was the primary driver in computer manufacture and innovation. They were far ahead of the competition, and their scale meant they were assumed to be untouchable.

So how come it was a small unknown company in Seattle, called Microsoft, that succeeded in cornering the desktop market?

Bill Gates was looking at the industry from a very different place.

Standing back from the apparent attraction of mainframe computers, he saw the potential impact of meeting the humbler needs of individuals, who could use some of that power in their everyday work and lives. He perceived the personal computing revolution before it happened.

No one sees everything, all of the time, but Bill Gates' qualities as a quiet disruptor have been evident for a long time. He has consistently prioritised thinking and reading time in his diary. As a result, he has a reputation for being one of the most widely read business leaders, bringing a depth and breadth of perception to all that he does. This now includes the global work of The Gates Foundation. Not bad for a software developer.

Increasingly, organisations of all types realise that they need to look further to understand the needs of their customers or stakeholders. No longer can they only come up with internal solutions to remain competitive or thrive.

This means cultivating a broader perspective.

Dr Rachel Naomi Remen talks about 'seeing from the edge'. She recognises the value in observing more and noticing things that others miss.

This has significantly impacted her work with people who have incurable conditions and helping them find a different level of wholeness and healing.

Her own experience of Crohn's disease both fuelled her passion in this area and enabled her to develop pioneering training for clinicians that went far beyond treating sickness. Her story is profound and inspiring, not just for doctors, but for all who trust that there are better answers.

And her core message? Listen generously.

So why do quiet disruptors tend to notice more and see with wider lenses?

Standing back from the issue is critical. Quiet disruptors are not motivated by finding the first answer, but the best solution. Therefore, they will take more time to reflect and consider the problem from multiple angles. This includes thinking about impact and implications probably longer and further than others.

Also, because they tend to see from the margins, they are more likely to be in observation mode.

Noticing things that others pass over, particularly in terms of intangibles issues, nuances of behaviour, or recognising groups or people outside of the mainstream. Listening generously is more likely to be in their toolkit (unless they get triggered by stimulating questions and go off in their heads!)

While quiet disruptors will have a focus on their passion, they also appear to have a breadth of interest. They are rarely narrow in what they consume and appear to be better at rejecting mere noise. This means their perception is likely to be widely informed and therefore of more substance.

Finally, there is the freedom which comes from not being wedded to the status quo.

This means they are more likely to see the cracks in current solutions and be prepared to offer more radical answers than others might venture.

Powerful insights

One of the reasons we don't have more insights is that we're looking in the wrong place.

Big data has wow-ed us so much that we think it's going to give us the next breakthrough. But insights aren't on a trajectory. They are a break from the trend.

Fundamentally, insights are a shift in our understanding of what is. Something causes us to see the familiar from a different angle, and as a result, we have a new story. One that can't be undone. We can't 'unsee' an insight, though not everyone gets it. At least initially.

The psychologist Gary Klein is well known for his work on insights. His book *Seeing What Others Don't: The Remarkable Ways We Gain Insights* unearths compelling stories about how individuals pursued their curiosity and found ways to break through seemingly impossible situations. Sometimes the consequences were specific to them personally, while others impact our lives every day from healthcare to flight and beyond.

Insights are unexpected; they come without warning and aren't explained by simple cause and effect. We can't just turn them on.

However, through Gary's work, we do know the tendencies that promote them:

- Noticing connections, coincidences and curiosities

- Responding to inconsistencies by looking at them from a different angle, even upside down

- Weeding out flawed beliefs

These can be expressed as habits of mind. And people who are quiet disruptors appear to cultivate these characteristics.

For example, quiet disruptors are more likely to have an actively curious mindset.

They are habitually asking questions, including 'where have I seen this before?', 'why is this happening?' This contrasts with those of us who just want to get on with the job in hand.

Quiet disruptors are also far more alert to the assumptions underpinning why we do what we do. And if these do not stack up, they will explore what happens if we change beliefs.

An example of weeding out flawed beliefs was Seth Godin's experience with the VisionSprings charity in India.

The people they encountered at the village stall doing the reading test required glasses and their visible money purses demonstrated that they had the cash to pay. But why were only a third purchasing?

The flawed assumption was that they would respond to the positive experience of choice like any other western consumer.

By removing the element of choice, they changed the story to 'Do you want us to take away what you have, or do you want to pay to keep the glasses that are already working for you?'

This change led to a 100% increase in the number of glasses purchased.

How good is that?

7

Interpreting complexity

Why do people do what they do?

Ultimately as humans, we make decisions and take actions that are consistent with how we see the world.

And even if things don't stack up, we create narratives that enable us to make sufficient sense to feel okay and operate on autopilot.

Unfortunately, recent history is littered with the failures of assuming we know how the world works. And the likelihood is that this is going to get worse—just taking the variable response to COVID-19 as an illustration.

Yet many still want to live in a relatively simple environment of known cause and effect, where life and work are predictable.

The problem is the world isn't like that anymore (if it ever was). Death remains the only certainty, and everything else is complex, unpredictable and ambiguous.

However, some people appear to navigate this new world better than others. These are people who are asking questions beyond the usual paradigm.

Looking for patterns

Warren Buffett of Berkshire Hathaway is a well-known investor, business magnate and philanthropist. He takes the long view in investing, looking for patterns and connections that only become apparent over time.

His capacity to make money is informed by his breadth and depth of view and is matched by his generosity as a philanthropist. It has also enabled him to survive multiple stock market crashes, learning ever more along the way.

There were other voices, too, who recognised the underlying problems with the global economy, like Meredith Whitney and Marcus Barry who saw what was happening in the sub-prime market in the mid noughties.

What they were saying challenged assumptions about the never-ending upward trajectory of property prices. Like Warren Buffett, they weren't loud voices, and they did their research, but those who heeded their challenge were not felled in the crash.

Seeing patterns and making connections across boundaries comes from asking more difficult questions. Those that challenge conventional wisdom.

Seeing the whole

Human factors is the study of the interactions between human beings and other elements of the systems in which they operate.

Professor Harold Thimbleby is a computer scientist and engineer by background. He started to become curious about human factors when looking at the pattern of errors with data entry on keypads.

Based at Swansea University, he now works globally in raising awareness of forced error in the design of medical devices, which has enormous human consequences. This is not only in terms of patient harm and even death, but also the blame that is too readily assigned to clinicians, particularly nurses, when things go wrong.

Unfortunately, the assumption is that the machine is always right, therefore any problems must be caused by human error. Harold's work has challenged this, in particular the bureaucratic handling of failure and the privileged position of device manufacturers. As a consequence, long-held assumptions are being questioned, and harm is being avoided.

Today a partial answer is only that: a partial answer. In the past, in our less interconnected and interdependent world, it might do as a proxy. But no more. We need to have a means of seeing the whole or at least the essential threads. And no single person can do this on their own, certainly not if they are using old lenses.

The Art of Perception is a program run by Amy E Herman, a consultant and educator with a background as a lawyer and artist historian.

Working with various law enforcement agencies, she uses group visits to galleries and museums to draw out the difference between looking and seeing. Collectively viewing well-known pieces of art enables the detectives to talk about what they see and change their perspective, leading to a shift in the way they observe and gather evidence in their day jobs.

When was the last time you stopped to reflect on the bigger picture or make connections that aren't immediately obvious in your team or organisation? What might you have missed along the way?

NEW EXPRESSIONS

'A mind once stretched by a new idea never regains its original dimensions'

OLIVER WENDELL BERRY

8

Releasing creativity

Blake Mycoskie had already started, run and sold four companies in his late teens and 20s before a trip to Argentina brought him face-to-face with poverty. Witnessing the impact of children growing up without shoes, he saw the potential to create a sustainable new solution, but not built on charity. TOMS shoes was born.

Buying a pair of TOMS shoes means buying into a radically different model of commerce. For each pair sold, another pair is given to a child in need. That is nearly 100 million pairs of shoes given away since 2006: One-for-One®

However, he hasn't stopped at creatively solving the need for shoes in impoverished countries. There is now TOMS Eyewear—which has restored sight to over 800,000 people since 2011—and TOMS Roasting Company, which provides a week's worth of safe drinking water for each bag of coffee sold (over 730,000 weeks' worth since 2014).

And there is more. But all based on a profitable entity with a radically creative business model. Seeing the world differently.

Creativity is vital, and it's much more than being able to draw, write or compose. The kind of world we live in and the complexity of the challenges we face require a very different way of finding solutions and enabling us to see and hear the way things really are.

Are we ready to cultivate and release the creativity that is already there?

Opening the box

One of the characteristics of the extraordinary season we are in has been the tangible release of creativity. Being more confined in our daily lives and being challenged by fundamental issues of humanity and personhood, has prompted many more to explore their dormant creative expression.

This urge to express ourselves is within all of us.

So why might we see this particularly in quiet disruptors?

Creativity is essentially the use of imagination and ideas to create something that hasn't had expression before.

For quiet disruptors, this is the opportunity to give outward expression to their rich inner dialogue, which may not have an existing language or vocabulary.

Our world has been turned upside down. Things that have been germinating for a while are coming to the surface. We need a new words for a new age.

Fresh expressions are the outcome. Whereas previously they may have been sat on, or starved of time and space to grow, people are now questioning what is really important to them—and having the courage to do something about it.

Yes, this can be messy territory. But whoever thought that new birth was neat and tidy?

9

Solving problems

'Imagination is more important than knowledge'
ALBERT EINSTEIN

If the answers were simple, we would have found them by now. And often quick and easy solutions come with unintended consequences, evident with hindsight.

However, the links between curiosity and creativity are well documented. By bringing fresh eyes, quiet disruptors have the potential to contribute genuinely new solutions. They also make and do existing things differently, with creativity that addresses broader issues.

New solutions

Genuine innovation, as opposed to refining what currently exists, often occurs when unlikely ideas or concepts are brought together. This might be achieved by bridging disciplines, breaking down silos or turning issues inside-out and seeing the challenges from a completely different angle.

But it starts with recognising that the current approach is inadequate, for whatever reason.

Curiosity and insight are powerful fuel for this kind of creativity. Asking very different types of questions, standing in someone else's shoes, making connections that aren't obvious. And doing so by leaning into the problem or issue with greater intent and empathy than is often the case

An example of this was in the early 2000's when we brought together a disparate group of clinicians, patients and others with a concern about the late identification of treatable eye problems in people with diabetes. From this, one of the first mobile digital diabetic retinopathy services in the world was born.

Damage to the retina was observable using existing technology, often before a person with diabetes would have even been aware of it. But this wasn't just a matter of technology. We needed to use a whole population approach and establish a rolling program that included everyone with a diagnosis of diabetes. Crucially this involved screening where they would naturally congregate not just telling them to go to the optician.

The program worked with GP surgeries, community centres and mosques across the whole of Berkshire and beyond (1 million population) achieving an extraordinarily high take-up rate. In the process, the sight of hundreds of people was saved, and we shifted the public conversation around diabetes.

A further sight-related story is that of Warby Parker, the company established by four college friends to address the problem of expensive glasses by combining dispensing with online retail. Adam Grant beautifully tells this story in *Originals: How Nonconformists Change the World*. It was such an unlikely success story that even Adam passed up the opportunity of investing—a big regret.

Making differently

Sometimes the creative solution is not a radically different model, but making something that is well known, differently, to achieve a more significant impact.

A delicious example of this is Askinosie Chocolate. Shawn Askinosie was a brilliant criminal defence lawyer. But he also knew that if he carried on, he would be dead. The workload and stress were unsustainable.

His quest for purposeful work that wouldn't kill him was a profound internal and external journey, which he shares in his book *Meaningful Work*. It took him deep inside himself and across the world to Africa and the Philippines in shaping his business vocation.

Askinosie Chocolate: 'It's not about the chocolate, it's about the chocolate.'

This wonderful, paradoxical statement sums up the tension of their vision:

> 'We at Askinosie Chocolate exist to craft exceptional chocolate whilst serving our farmers, our customers, our neighbourhood, and one another, striving in all we do to leave whatever part of the world we touch better for the encounter.'

Shawn's chocolate is ranked with the best, winning awards globally. But the impact they make on the ground is equally as impressive. The real partnership with farmers in Tanzania, Ecuador and the Philippines includes innovative open-book management and profit-sharing direct trade. It extends to community development in their local schools, to secure their future without donations, and a proper exit strategy.

And the local partnerships in Springfield, Missouri are touching many lives with dignity and hope.

Askinosie Chocolate: 'tastes good, does good.' They can only do this if they not only make excellent chocolate but are also profitable, earning enough to fulfil their vocation. And this is the whole point.

Doing differently

Courageous creativity not only enables quiet disruptors to make things differently, but it also provides scope to re-imagine doing everyday things to generate radically improved outcomes.

There is a groundswell of clinicians who have simply 'had enough'. Their endeavours to practice more person-centred care is an uphill struggle. They know that healthcare needs a fundamental revolution.

Coming together for stimulus and encouragement to keep going, they are finding ways to share novel approaches. This includes *The Journal of Health Design*, led by a multinational, multidisciplinary editorial board including doctors, other clinical practitioners and academics and innovators in design.

One of the current research projects is called *The Big Chair*. It stems from the curiosity and empathy of its editor-in-chief, Dr Moyez Jiwa, about what happens when you shift the balance of power in the GP consultation. The small shift in offering the incoming patient the doctor's chair made a significant change in the clinical conversation and the consequence of the consultation. This included the likelihood that the patient would follow the advice and prescriptions offered and their sense of satisfaction with the experience.

Even thinking about the question of who sits in the doctor's chair requires courageous creativity, because it contrasts so sharply with established norms in health-care. These things that clinicians and patients do without thinking that reinforces a mindset that is unhelpful and even counterproductive.

Remembering too, the impact of inviting would-be change-makers to a cowshed in West Wales—for The Do Lectures—and the avalanche of courageous creativity it has released over the last eleven years as a result.

Perhaps one of the dimensions of this aptitude for new ideas stems from a mindset that sees possibilities and the potential for abundance rather than being fixated by short-term scarcity. Fired by hope and powered by conviction.

10

Creative encounters

'Creativity takes courage.'

Henri Matisse was an artist and rebel with a reputation for propelling the art world from impressionism and post-impressionism to modernity. He understood courage and creativity.

Not only can quiet disruptors creatively help us uncover new solutions, they also help us encounter the world around us from a different perspective. This is where creativity and creative expression helps us to see, hear and experience things beyond our usual frame. And causes us to shift and take action.

This disruption either *pulls* us toward change, by enabling us to encounter the familiar differently through offering us fresh sight. Or it *pushes* us towards change, by giving voice to others so that we can hear them, disturbing our sense of normality.

Fresh sight

The power of the visual is enormous. Think about the iconic images that have changed our perception of the world around us.

The young girl fleeing napalm bombing in Vietnam. The first-ever image of the whole Earth, taken from the moon orbit. The euphoria of the Berlin Wall being breached. Or the power of David Attenborough's *Blue Planet* documentaries graphically demonstrating the effect of our discarded plastic waste on the oceans, and his 2020 film *A Life on Our Planet.* These shift our sense of where we are, who we are, and what we might become.

The street artist known as Banksy is probably the most visible quiet disruptor in this space currently. He is known for his extraordinary images and how he chooses to display them.

As an artist, he is intentionally invisible and amplifies that paradox with calculated irony to make his point.

His Walled-Off Hotel (say it quickly and you'll get it) in the Palestinian West Bank, in Bethlehem, is probably his most immersive work. It invites people into an art-filled, exquisitely crafted environment. Here perceptions of the way things are nudged to make way for a more open, inclusive understanding of reality, fed by experience and exposure, not dogma.

Others lend us their eyes, ears and voices to encounter the world in a new way. For example, music or songs that have drawn us into an environment of courage and hope.

Or the cartoonists who enable us to have a fresh take, often at multiple levels. People like Bill Watterson with *Calvin and Hobbes*, or Scott Adams and *Dilbert*. These simple drawings enable us to laugh at ourselves and have more honest conversations in a less threatening way. Currently, I'm enjoying the *Gapingvoid* blog: cartoons and comment as a dose of reality.

These opportunities for fresh sight speak without words and become part of us, almost without noticing. Powerfully permeating our perspective, because they start by seeing things differently.

New Art

One of the characteristics of the emerging expressions is the merging of media. Not only do the astonishing advances in technology open up greater creative expressions, but artists are questioning more.

This is fertile ground for thoughtful creatives because they have both a creative imagination, and the tools to push boundaries.

An example of this is the work of Alexa Meade.

At the point of deciding what to do after graduation, Alexa took the extraordinary step of radically pursuing her creative curiosity, when a bright future in public policymaking would have been her's for the taking.

Her fascination with shadows led to her highly creative and experimental art installations. Imagining 3D as 2D—people as paintings—she started experimenting with painting herself.

As she says at the end of her 2016 TED talk:

> '... you can find the strange in the familiar, as long as you are willing to look beyond what's already been brought to light; that you can see what's below the surface, including the shadows, and recognise that there can be more than meets the eye...'
>
> ALEXA MEADE

Leslie Holt is a different kind of artist. Identifying with quiet disruption, she uses her fine art training and blends painting with other media, including embroidery. For example, her Neuro Blooms project: 'Making mental health conditions visible and beautiful...'

Did you know that many common mental health conditions have distinctive brain patterns when seen through PET scanning? In bringing these differences to light through her work, Leslie not only gives expression to things not usually seen but also gives voice to those suffering in this way.

Her series of enamel pins, developed in collaboration with Shiny Apple Studio, has prompted the start of many brave conversations. Neuro Blooms has been popular, particularly among young adults, the age at which mental illness often begins.

And there are many more visual artists, filmmakers, photographers, who are making emotional connections in their work and quietly disrupting our view of how the world is.

Creative activism

Quiet disruption is also expressed through a different kind of activism. One that doesn't rely on aggressive volume or numbers. But instead creatively connects with those whose opinions they want to change, person-to-person, instead of crowd-to-title.

Sarah Corbett has extensive experience as a professional activist in the traditional sense, including with international charities such as Oxfam. However, she started exploring a different way using 'creativity to make the public aware of the struggles people are still going through'.

In 2009 Sarah formed the Craftism Collective as a social enterprise to engage people in social justice issues 'in a quiet, non-confrontational manner involving pretty, handcrafted gestures of defiance.'

One of her early campaigns in 2016 was making individual, beautifully gift-wrapped, embroidered handkerchiefs for each member of the Marks & Spencer plc board to advocate for their being early adopters of the National Living Wage in the UK. The chair of the board acknowledged that the effect was more profound than any large-scale demonstration would have achieved and resulted in a sea change in policy for the retailer, impacting thousands of low-paid workers.

Who could have imagined the impact of simple needlework? Yet this has enabled many people to find their voice and express their convictions.

The act of crafting a gift or banner requires thoughtful presence. It isn't a hurried act or mass-produced. As a result, a different emotional connection is forged. In many instances, this has enabled a shift from confrontation to a level of collaborative and honest conversation. With extraordinary results.

This is the courage to speak softly and creatively about things that matter.

And change the conversation.

11

Words that explode

We are going through such a tumultuous shift that we do need a new language. The words that we have used are tired and stale. They trap us in what was.

However, this new language starts with a groan. A yearning that doesn't immediately have expression.

It feels alien and at times, overwhelming. And in our fear, we are tempted to turn away. But we need to resist.

At these times, those who sit with this anguish long enough to shape it into words are our travelling companions.

These are the new change-makers. Let's welcome them.

'Finally comes the poet'

I was captivated by this beautiful Walt Whitman line in *Leaves of Grass* when I first came across it years ago as a book title. I appreciated the book, but the phrase endured.

What is it about poetry that gets under our skin? That moves us to open up, to step outside and beyond ourselves in a way that surprises us?

Perhaps it's the gaps between the words, the space for our imagination and motivation. The way the poet doesn't attempt to nail it all down, precisely. Allowing the words to breathe, in a rhythm that disturbs our internal clock. And metaphors that explode our sight.

Poems challenge the narrowness of our rationality and invite us to enter into experience rather than knowledge. They touch emotions we may have long closed down and remind us what it is to be human, reconnecting us to ourselves and others.

Much of our timeless, great literature—across all cultures—is poetic in nature. Poems and metaphors transcend. So it is not surprising that those who want to stimulate change often look beyond convincing arguments or loud noise.

"I have a dream..." was one of the most potent phrases of the 20th century

Today we are in in the midst of an explosion of poetry. Have you noticed?

Creative citizenship

Roger Robinson, who won the 2019 TS Eliot poetry prize, coined the phrase 'creative citizenship' to express the invitation that poetry can offer. He was introduced to the idea of Creative Citizenships by Professor Henry Mainsah and made the idea central to his art practice. This way to engage with things that are human and give voice to our connectedness. Our mutual obligation to see and name.

His poetry cuts through the defences we have erected to protect our view of the world. Not through violence, but by creating a bridge that we allow ourselves to cross. Because it connects with our humanity and gives us hope in our vulnerability. Sometimes by laughing at ourselves.

And through it, we hear the other voice.

Roger's work using poetry has enabled powerful community-wide conversations, including about the Grenfell Tower disaster in London, and the Windrush scandal in the UK.

And he is not alone.

Across every continent, thoughtfully creative writers are giving voice to the injustice, inequality, environmental destruction and other issues that call for us to stand up as citizens of the world.

Expressing things that are difficult to grapple with unless we have a different language.

It's time to hear them and enter the conversation.

Speaking up differently

The voice of the poet is also starting to be heard in the heart of our organisations.

Poets like Parker Palmer and David Whyte speak to the essence of what we are doing together. Creating space to explore meaning, connections and leadership through an entirely different lens.

Especially in our ambiguous, complex and interconnected world, we need a different language for sensemaking. Logical dialogue is too tight and tidy. Poetry and metaphor help us discuss what is really happening beneath the transient noise and old solutions.

Its value is evidenced in well-known businesses and consulting organisations who are now using poetry in their leadership and organisational development work.

And then there's Gideon Heugh.

Gideon is a young poet who also works for Tearfund, a UK humanitarian charity. In a sector living daily in extremes of human suffering, where words have been used as battering rams on our emotions and we are fatigued in the hearing, his poetry takes us on a new path.

Not skirting the challenges, his poetry draws us in, graciously and powerfully. And enables us to be fellow travellers with fresh eyes.

Storytelling

Along with poetry, including the dramatic rise of spoken word poetry, storytelling is emerging as a cultural form of this age.

It also offers a powerful means of sensemaking, both of who we are as individuals and communities, and our wider world.

Stories invite us into a narrative where we can see ourselves. It connects our emotions and experience, not just our minds.

Because amid dislocation, people want to belong.

For quiet disruptors, storytelling provides a persona to inhabit and a medium to use that enables them to be heard in a noisy world more familiar with shouting. Because when people participate in a story, they know they are entering a new landscape, that invites a different kind of attention.

Beginnings, middles and endings are expected. And therefore the sense of time and immediate judgement are often suspended. We are waiting for the conclusion and get immersed in a different world along the way.

Storytellers are speaking to us and speaking on our behalf. They allow us to explore unfamiliar territory in a familiar way and in doing so, creatively open our eyes.

Led by Prue Thimbleby, the first two *International Storytelling for Health* conferences were held in Wales in 2017 and 2019. Exploring this powerful medium for sensemaking for both patients and clinicians cut through established assumptions about what is needed, from childbirth through to death and dying.

The impact has been astonishing and liberating. And people are feeling heard.

COURAGEOUS CONNECTIONS

'Courage is found in unlikely places'

JRR TOLKIEN

12

Shaping culture

While you probably wouldn't expect quiet disruptors to be the life and soul of the party, they are good to have around.

People warm to Brené Brown. They listen to her TED Talks, watch her in conversation, or hear a podcast. This isn't a woman who shies away from telling it like it is, and she takes people with her.

In doing so, they find the bravery to encounter themselves and each other with more courage and vulnerability. Extraordinary. And she's a quiet disruptor.

Over years of walking an unconventional path, Brené has found her voice and is comfortable in her skin. She has spoken to multitudes in public, and she is still nervous. Every time.

And in her writing, she displays the same no-BS that she applies to herself and her work.

The latest book *Dare to Lead – Brave Work, Tough Conversations, Whole Hearts* is the summation of all her work. This is two decades of grounded theory research and application through Brave Leaders Inc.

It was triggered by the universal responses from senior leaders to the question: what is required now? 'We need braver leaders and more courageous cultures.' The reasons why spanned the need for critical thinking, building trust, inspiring innovation, finding common ground, making tough decisions and the importance of empathy and relationship building.

These issues speak face-on to the emerging world. And because of their aptitude, quiet disruptors have an increasing role in meeting these needs and shaping the kind of courageous culture that Brené inspires.

At Basecamp, the trailblazing software company founded by Jason Fried and David Heinemeier Hansson 20 years ago, they deliberately shaped a different kind of culture. Building a way of working that celebrates calm in multiple dimensions and releases better productivity, completely bucking the trend. *It Doesn't Have to be Crazy at Work* is their manifesto.

These ideas contrast sharply with Gary Hamel's findings about the global state of company culture in recent years. The statistics are staggering.

According to Gary's 2019 research:

- Only 13% of employees around the world are emotionally engaged in their work

- 79% of respondents from large companies said new ideas get greeted with scepticism or hostility

- 76% said political behaviours highly influence who gets ahead

- The average first-level employee in large organisations is buried under eight or more layers of management

It's sobering.

Life

But our culture is vastly more than organisations and work. It's our lives and how we live them together.

How do we choose to recognise and see each other? What frames our social and cultural norms?

Culture is like the air we breathe or the water we swim in. It's largely invisible to us most of the time. It's what we take for granted and assume to be the same for everyone.

It gets stuck in cycles of behaviour, and we stop seeing the triggers, or the fact that it could be different.

This time of disruption has shown us that change is more possible than we had dared to believe. And changing culture is the key.

So why do I believe that quiet disruptors can help to shape the kind of culture that we need to thrive in this new era?

The previous chapters have highlighted some of their specific qualities of curiosity and creativity. But they bring more than capabilities and characteristics. They have the potential to infuse and grow the way we do things together, for the better.

They dare to speak softly about things that matter. Making courageous connections and then doing something about it.

13

Organisational conscience

'A lot of people never use their initiative because no-one told them to...'

BANKSY, WALL AND PIECE, 1988

What causes some people to step up and speak out? Ultimately, it's because their passion or conviction outweighs their fear. They are compelled to, even if it costs them.

One of the distinguishing characteristics of quiet disruptors is being prepared to leave the comfort of their natural internal space for the sake of the cause. To take action and challenge the way things are because they see a better way.

Quiet disruptors are not armchair pundits. However, they don't always find an easy way to express themselves and are frequently misunderstood. It may take time to find and develop their voice.

For a number, this is speaking up differently, often from the side-lines. Using their creative capacity to enable things that are important to be heard: the prophetic voice. And finding a different medium for activism than fighting or shouting.

It can also be within our organisations, institutions or community where their questioning can sift out what is really important. Or hold those in power to account.

Shifting the conversation

Simon Sinek, Susan Cain and Brené Brown have all shifted the conversation, each in their own way. This includes in the specific organisations they have worked with and in the general atmosphere.

Start With Why has given a language to leaders and organisations that shifts the focus from what they are doing, or how they are doing it, to what is their purpose. Simply by asking the question, it has enabled many to connect more deeply to both their endeavours and who they want to impact. As a result, those within the organisation often have a greater sense of meaning. And it's clearer where they add value.

When you know why you are doing what you are doing, you are more open to finding better and more creative ways of doing it. And it's much easier to have a conversation about better solutions when the identity of the group or organisation isn't tied to an existing way of doing things. There is a higher calling.

And there is a longer-term view. In *The Infinite Game*, Simon articulates the urgency of shifting our gaze from a 'win or lose' mentality to one which sees our endeavours within the long arc of history. Not as a binary choice, but a call to play the long game. With huge consequences.

All this is evidenced in the organisations Simon has worked with and influenced as a global thought leader.

Likewise for Brené Brown. Only the brave invite her in because she talks about things like emotions, courage and vulnerability, in the same breath as leading fearlessly.

Yes, these are big names, and their reach is in person and through their work. But at a smaller scale, both leaders who themselves are quiet disruptors, and where teams give space for the thoughtful change-makers, the conversation also shifts.

There is a better balance between long and short-term talking.

Currently, in many organisations, the reactive, tactical agenda wins every time, until people lose sight of the underpinning reason why they are there. *Any* action becomes a substitute for good action, and no one calls it out. No one really knows how far off course they are because they are still moving, aren't they? And that's the metric.

Better meetings

The typical meeting culture amplifies this passive thinking further. Many people are spending virtually all of their contracted time in formal and informal meetings. But meetings are rarely where the real work happens. And the ROI—return on investment—isn't even considered.

Quiet disruptors would be much more likely to ask why we are meeting, what we are trying to achieve and probing the best way of getting there. However, that takes more thinking, which we are not used to because doing is valued more highly. 'Say no to meetings' is an uncomfortable challenge, which only the brave would utter.

However, with more thoughtful meeting planning—probably fewer and shorter meetings, with better agendas and a more explicit focus on outcomes—quiet disruptors can make more valuable contributions. This is where their deeper, reflective thinking and willingness to question the status quo brings real benefits to the conversation. But ask them reactively, in the moment, and you'll miss all this.

The influence of quiet disruptors also helps to counteract groupthink. We are all subject to our cultural worldviews, though we rarely recognise them. Increasing complexity, uncertain environments, and fewer clear-cut answers mean we are more likely to suffer from unseen biases in our thinking and talking.

Without a challenge to the prevailing narrative, teams and organisations can think and talk themselves into dangerous waters without realising it. The litany of high-profile failures—from well-established corporate giants like RBS and Lehmann Brothers, through to humanitarian Non-Governmental Organisations (NGOs) like Oxfam—over the last decade often demonstrate the effects of groupthink.

We need to shift the ground in our conversations. Avoiding rocking the boat is no longer an option if we want our organisations or work to thrive. We need more conversations at the boundary.

Speaking out

Catherine Howarth is on a mission, and she wants 'deeds not words.'

As CEO of ShareAction, the NGO that coordinates civil society activists to promote responsible investment across Europe, Catherine is passionate about real social responsibility in investment organisations to make the world safer for people and the planet.

In 2018 activist investors challenged Shell, the Anglo-Dutch oil conglomerate, to reconsider its projected investment in green energy. The result was a doubling of its planned investment up to $4bn after 2020. In calling out the conflict between Shell's climate policy and its corporate lobby, but doing so in a way that demonstrated belief in investment as a force for good, these activists persuaded major investors to back the call.

One of ShareAction's most significant achievements in recent years was the change to UK pension fund trustee regulations. These regulations now require public disclosure on how funds are factoring environmental and social risk management in their investment processes. Pension funds are enormous—far more substantial than many of us realise—and the impact of where they are invested has significant long-term consequences.

Disrupting corporate decision-making like this requires both clarity of purpose and taking the long view, including carefully building its reputation.

Every day there are many examples of where thoughtful and creative change-makers act as our conscience. People on boards who ask questions that go beneath the surface, or call attention to inconsistencies in approach. Team members who clarify the consequences of proposals and offer an alternative. Those who, in whatever way, take a stand and say this is a line they will not cross because it matters.

We also need people to help us 'see the wood for the trees'.

Quiet disruptors are more likely to stand back and see the whole, rather than be caught up in the details of the parts. And because they take the long view—often from the edge rather than the middle—they may be more able to see when we are a degree or two off course.

This is discretionary effort. Often they are not paid to do this, but it matters to them. And therefore they are more alert to the consequences. But because they don't shout, you may not always hear them, unless you take the time to listen.

14

Joining the dots

It is usually from the boundary that we have a better view. From here quiet disruptors see potential connections more clearly, and more significant opportunities for fruitful collaboration.

Natural curiosity and motivation to find creative solutions means that they are likely to spend more energy outside of the proverbial box than some of their colleagues. And they may be better at asking open questions, which leads to places that others might not go.

Informally, this means that quiet disruptors are likely to be aware of what is happening more widely in the organisation or community, and with customers and stakeholders. It is part of how they make sense of what they are doing.

They are also less likely to be threatened by collaboration, finding opportunities to learn from and with others because it serves the greater good.

In seeing the whole, quiet disruptors will be more likely to advocate for joining the dots and breaking down silos. They will do this with less force and aggression, taking people with them by persuasion.

Because you don't have to shout to make a change. And if people feel seen and heard they are more open to cross their bridges and join in.

Generous connections

Bernadette Jiwa is a soft-spoken business philosopher and marketing strategist. She delights in enabling people to do work they are proud of through brand storytelling. And her faint Dublin accent, carried across the world working with entrepreneurs and business leaders, evidences her storytelling roots. Beautifully.

Connecting our story with the story of those we seek to serve creates generous and meaningful connections. Bernadette demonstrates this through her work and writing, and the way she gathers people together. She knows how to create the right kind of space for them to step out and make a difference.

Because, as she says, 'you don't need to compete when you know who you are.'

Less well-known is the story of Moneypenny, the first virtual assistant service in the UK. Rachel Clacher and brother Ed Reeves were both artists but in different locations. Endeavouring to arrange transportation of Ed's paintings ready for display, they couldn't be in multiple places at the same time. They needed someone they could trust to handle calls on their behalf.

Broken promises and rigid responses later, they recognised the need and set up a service that would treat others how they would want to be treated themselves. To do this, they recruited for attitude, not just aptitude, and focused on getting the small things right. This included approaching business from the other end and empowering their PAs to identify what would make the service better for their clients, and frontline staff.

> 'Make good promises and stick to them... Wear other people shoes... And communicate all the time... Challenge the process to do the right thing... Make better mistakes...'

Rachel is a classic quiet disruptor and walks the talk. I've loved seeing how she has grown the business and the people in it—and has been recognised along the way.

Changing the world

Given that conviction runs deep for many quiet disruptors, we should not be surprised to see them wanting to change the world. Or at least their part of the globe.

Just because they are thoughtful and rarely shout, doesn't mean there is a limit to their ambition.

Take Jacqueline Novogratz, the founder and chief executive of the Acumen Fund: a global community of socially and environmentally responsible entrepreneurs and investors dedicated to changing the way the world tackles poverty. Her curiosity, determination and sense of justice fires her quest for a better way to do good in the world.

She joins the dots not by having the answers to everything, but by learning how to grow people and ideas that radically transform communities. Not through charity, but making the connection through enterprise. Backing others and walking with them, developing a *Manifesto for a Moral Revolution* that transcends cultures and gives backbone to those who push through against the odds to stand with the poor. And see millions of lives and thousands of communities radically changed, with a sustainable future.

Shared questions

One of the ways that quiet disruptors join the dots is through their habit of asking questions. Prod below the surface and you'll find why? what if...? and how can we? fuelling their thinking.

Harold Thimbleby's thinking about the design of data entry systems for medical devices took him to the safety culture in aviation and beyond. He upturns our sense of how things are by bringing together insights from multiple disciplines to frame laser-sharp questions that drive change. And yes, they are uncomfortable.

Dr Moyez Jiwa's experience of the immigration system as a child enabled him to completely re-think the patient-doctor relationships in both medical education and clinical practice. By questioning *why-we-do-what-we-do* from a different angle and involving others, he offers a radical alternative that is changing outcomes at both an individual and community level.

While quiet disruptors might have already covered a lot of ground in their internal thinking, they know the power of opening up the question.

Amos Doornbos is a Dutch-Canadian living in the UK. Involved in digital transformation in global humanitarian aid, his questions are shaped by experience in the field and transferring insights from vastly different contexts. Like other quiet disruptors, he takes us to places where we see things differently, unpicking our assumptions and shifting what we think is our role in making change. And these are things we can't unlearn.

Perhaps the most potent questioner I know is Krista Tippett. Her ferocious generosity is matched by her thirst for wisdom about how we can make the world a better place. Krista's *On Being Podcast* is a masterclass in making connections with questions. And these are not small questions, neither are they time-bound. Instead, they lodge like a little pebble in a shoe. Timeless reminders about what is vital for living our life here on this planet and how we choose to be together.

15

Inspiring hope

'Great change leaders put their knowledge to the background and their presence to the foreground.'

Wise words from Deborah Rowland, researcher, consultant and author of *Still Moving: How to Lead Mindful Change.*

Hope and a sense of calm are caught, not taught. To be real and lasting, it resides in our heart and soul, not our heads. Therefore, how we show up has far more of an impact than most of us realise.

Dr Rachel Naomi Remen has effected significant change in the doctor-patient culture by her clinical practice and her teaching about listening generously. But to do this, she had to come to the place of accepting that she was a wounded healer. Not rejecting the pain of her condition, but instead using it to inspire hope that people with chronic and life-limiting conditions can be healed, even if their sickness can't be cured.

This is not a culture of strength and status, but the calm vulnerability of being alongside. She knew that doctors, too, needed to have this experience of being listened to for themselves if they had any chance of offering it to their patients. Without this, for many their tendency is to create a protective shell.

Creating space

Quiet disruptors, whether as a leader or team member, naturally bring space with them. It's what they do when they are at their best.

However, this isn't a negative absence, but the potential for gracious generosity. They don't have to fill every gap, always take control, or talk the loudest. Though if they get pushed into a corner, they will probably stop talking completely.

And the identity of a quiet disruptor isn't wrapped up in being a superhero, so they don't generally provoke dogfights.

Instead, they often help cut through the tangled mess of the immediate, to see the bigger picture and make better sense of what is going on. They will celebrate how far we've come, only raising the alarm if it's necessary to get us out of danger. There is hope.

For some people, though, quiet disruptors are too slow or deep, and that can feel threatening. And they won't always be the one to lead change. But in most situations we don't need the fastest responses, but the best.

A frenetic culture burns itself out, eventually.

Sightlines

Sometimes the hope that quiet disruptors can inspire comes from their natural view from the edge. Seeing more than the immediate, they point to what's coming—the proverbial light at the end of the tunnel or the sunrise on the horizon.

It is coming. There is an after.

Quiet disruptors also offer the sense of 'we are not alone.' By seeing who else is working in an area, they can encourage hope that a way can be found. Or make the connection for synergy to occur.

By offering 'did you know that...' in a way that is not testing or controlling, we grow each other. This is a big shift from 'knowledge is power', to 'there's a world of abundance' if we choose to see it that way.

And these sightlines are getting bigger and longer. Since we are no longer confined by how much we know, nor by where we are based.

Being seen

We all want to be seen and heard. It validates our identity and strengthens our hope.

Quiet disruptors are unlikely to be the warmest or cuddliest of people around, but they do notice. That observation could also mean picking up when something is not right, as well as when there is a positive change.

People are less likely to be hidden in the crowd or ignored because they are different when quiet disruptors are around.

Over time this gives others more confidence to use their voice and express an opinion. Especially for other quiet disruptors, whose voice might be different from the majority.

And they do listen and may be less likely to talk over us.

Yes, there are times when something that is said sparks other thoughts and connections, and they drift off into their heads. And stop being present. But they do come back, usually, and take what you've said and build on it further.

In an era which is characterised by time pressure and distraction overload, being heard is rare. Yet it is a core part of being human, and without it, we are diminished.

As Rachel Naomi Remen exhorts: 'listen generously'.

'Me' to 'We'

The final dimension of how quiet disruptors can inspire hope and change the culture is their orientation to move the conversation from 'me' to 'we'.

When I think about the many people referred to in this book as quiet disruptors, their language is a healthy mix of 'me' and 'we'. They know who they are and what they stand for. They don't merge into the background. Yet neither is it all about them.

They own their voice, often working against the tide in the prevailing culture, but they don't shout. And some-times they can be uncomfortable to have around because they don't say 'yes' just to keep the peace.

However, it's not their empire they are building. That's not where their values lie. Instead, quiet disruptors are often heralding a way to make 'stronger together' a re-ality. Because they can see the possibilities and know it will take all of us to get there.

But if they are pushed against a wall, their language will be a more defensive 'I'. Yet give them space and their blossoming is a collective bloom, where difference is celebrated, and title and status are less important than contribution.

In the emerging new normal, this is more important than ever. We all need a sense of hope and meaning.

Just don't put quiet disruptors in a box.

PART 3: CHANGE THE CONVERSATION

16

Become the change

'It takes courage to show up and become who you really are.'

E E CUMMINGS

When we think about the people who have made the most positive disruption in our world, it is rarely those with a megaphone.

Neither is it those who simply told us what to do or drew diagrams for us to follow.

Instead, these are people who have embodied the change they seek to make and have stepped forward—learning as they go and gathering people with them.

None of these—from Nelson Mandela and Gandhi through to Greta Thunberg and Brené Brown—arrived on the scene as fully formed change-makers.

That's why I believe it is far more helpful to think in terms of *becoming* the change, rather than trying to *be* the change.

We don't just decide; we permit ourselves to grow. Otherwise, we might become discouraged and give up.

Along the way, three dimensions help us step up from intention to fruitfulness in becoming thoughtful and creative change-makers, who make a difference in our work and world:

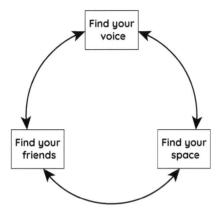

This isn't a linear process, but instead cycles of discovery. While there's no right place to start, getting stuck on one is like expecting to thrive on a diet of chocolate. There are consequences.

The next three chapters are more like a handbook, offering bite-sized practical insights and suggestions to help you develop. Take your time, and dip in and out as you need. In one sense this is the work of a lifetime.

Of course, we still have the cross the threshold, and the final short chapter helps us navigate our way over, with a personal blessing on our endeavours.

Enjoy the journey of becoming.

17

Find your friends

As human beings, we are fundamentally social and relational creatures. While you might not rush into the middle of a crowd, being completely isolated is an unhealthy place to be.

We flourish when we feel heard and seen. And if we are bringing a message—in whatever form—that others may not grasp at first pass, then knowing there is at least someone who is rooting for us is huge.

They don't have to understand everything. They just have to believe in us and be prepared to ask the hard questions. To help us get back on our feet when we trip up. And remind us that this is a journey, not a race.

Sometimes, these are long-term close friends. But there are also opportunities to 'find the others' for a period, online and elsewhere.

Being with them makes a difference. It gives us the confidence to stretch, to step out and grow. To try things out, knowing there is a safety net. Because these are people who want us to become all that we can be. And more.

In 2018 I had a dawning realisation that I had become too isolated. I was drying up and needed to do something about it. Two vibrant online communities and a change of church community later, I realise just how vital this relational dimension is.

It underpins everything else because we are not designed to be alone. Even the most introverted amongst us.

Don't wait until you become shrivelled before taking action. Even if it involves physically moving.

'Find the others.'

This is the brilliant refrain from Seth Godin in the Akimbo workshops. In his passion for encouraging and equipping people to 'go make a ruckus', he recognises the fundamental importance of human connection.

I suspect that for anyone who stands out, who appears to lead the charge for real change, that there are others. Those few who also 'get' the issue. Who share the idea, and who offer their support in multiple ways.

Where are they?

Find the others

Tribes build sideways.

And the connection economy depends on that simple truth. If you care about something, you must not wait for someone in charge to organise everyone else who cares about it.

I'm not sure if Timothy Leary understood the urgency of his words. Today, when it's easier and faster to connect people who are waiting to be connected, inaction is the same thing as opposition.

Ten by ten by ten is a thousand. Do it twice and you're at a million.

SETH'S BLOG, JANUARY 20, 2015

It's no longer about putting an ad in the newspaper and waiting for the post to arrive.

Shooting in the dark and wondering if there's anyone out there.

Our potential for connection travels both the people route (current estimates for degrees of separation are at three and falling) and the information highway. Search engines are powerful if used thoughtfully.

Who are the people who share your interests and perspectives? What can you learn from them, and what can you contribute?

Where do the people like you congregate, in person and virtually?

If these are folk who are at the sharp end—those on the edge, the change-makers who aren't content with the offering in the middle—then there probably won't be many.

But they *are* there. And you need to find them.

Not always to formally join forces, but to at least have a human reference point. To know that you are seen and heard.

Therefore, even if it's an uphill struggle to change the conversation and talk about things that are important, you still know that there are others who understand you.

Building generous communities

With the internet, we have the opportunity to do more than wave at a distance. We can build communities with generous intent. Being with people who strengthen our courage to speak softly about things that matter.

In my experience, the accent is on the quality of the community. What is the balance between being self-serving and genuinely enabling others to flourish? Because if the latter is the foundation, then everyone grows. It is organically transformative, not just transactional.

When you see or experience this in operation, the effect is profound. But it's not what we often encounter, and it's a million miles away from the usual networking activity.

Those who have been to The Do Lectures, whether in person or the online workshops, talk about their experience in these terms. So do those who have participated in any of the Akimbo workshops with Seth Godin, or *the* Right Company with Bernadette Jiwa. And there are more — both online and in person.

'People like us do things like this...'

And it's contagious.

There are also smaller steps that you could take right now to find the others and start building a community online. For example:

- Blogs—taking time to hear someone share their passion and perspective is a good way to find the others. Expand your repertoire and see who you find.

- Creating—you also can start writing or creating and sharing yourself. Generously and consistently showing up for others. Yes, it takes time, and it feels awkward at first, unleashing our imposter syndrome. But it will also help you find your voice and connect with the others who are encouraged by what they hear from you.

- Podcasts—have a similar principle to blogs, and they are mushrooming. It's a fantastic new world, and it certainly crosses borders.

- Social media—yes this is the last on the list and probably should be approached with wisdom as it can be a noisy and draining distraction. However, if used thoughtfully and selectively, it can also build generous communities.

Finally, there are many ways in which we can build with others in person whether that's discovering people in our workplaces and local areas or responding to opportunities to join in wider communities of purpose.

Some of the stories earlier in the book may have sparked your interest. Or you may find the suggestions for finding your voice coming next will stir a desire to find the others.

If so, take it seriously. You need them, and they need you.

18

Find your voice

Our voice is much more than how we sound.

It's what we have to say and the way we choose to express it. It changes over time. And yes, sometimes we have to intentionally dig it out because it's become buried in layers of should, ought, fear and shame.

This is about releasing what is already there, within you. Not going off and finding a new one!

In becoming the change we want to see, many avenues can help us explore our voice with confidence:

- Find your story

- Find your courage

- Find your tone

- Find your rhythm

- Find your medium

Think of this as a tasting menu. There is a lot you can explore further. These are simply pointers to munch on, and make notes as you go.

And take your time, enjoy the exploration. This isn't a race or a test. And it will probably be here in some form for the rest of your life.

Find your story

We all love a good story. It takes us on an emotional journey, helps us connect with others, and make sense of the world around us.

Our own story is crucial in helping us find our voice—the real me and what makes me tick.

Without it, we're just copying someone else, and it's shallow, empty and doesn't ring true. Or we struggle to find the right words or actions, fearful that we might get it wrong—because it's not essentially us—it's someone else's story.

We need to know *why* the change we want to see is so important to us, not just what it looks like.

1. Who am I?

As Bernadette Jiwa helpfully reminds us: 'When you know who you are you don't have to compete.'

So who were you before someone told you who you should be?

This isn't about creating but revealing your identity. And that means being honest with yourself and others.

Letting go of things that were put on you, perhaps for the best of intentions, but really don't fit.

2. What brings me joy?

Shawn Askinosie talks about 'gathering your prouds and celebrating your vocation.'

When you look back over your life, what are the moments you are proud of? Or when you felt profound joy and satisfaction?

Are there clues here?

3. Where were my 'diamonds' formed?

Again, there is great learning from Shawn's story. He recognised that the place where diamonds are formed is in the 'crucible of pains'.

Things that affect us deeply not only shape who we are but also motivate us to make a difference.

What are you holding in your hands or heart, that few others will have ever experienced?

4. What is the me shaped hole in the world?

For years I have carried a phrase from Rob Bell around with me, about '...being open to your role in the ongoing creation of the world....'

This is a powerful invitation to find the space that only you can occupy. Doing what only you can do by being who you are. Honestly and fully.

Only you can be you. And you have a distinctive contribution to make. You just might not have recognised it yet...

5. What pushes my buttons?

Passion and sensitivity are close cousins. These are the things that frequently trigger our emotions and speak volumes.

Where do your triggers show up? Are there situations that make you feel particularly excited or, conversely, rejected?

These aren't always big things and maybe are about how we handle what happens around us, in our everyday lives. Over time patterns emerge, but we don't always notice them. Until we do...

Find your courage

There's a big difference between seeing what could be different and doing something about it—speaking up and changing the conversation.

Where we find our courage has a significant part to play. And it will be different for each of us.

1. What naturally paralyses me?

This is swimming against our own tide. Knowing what frequently blocks me is key to unlocking my bravery.

We all gravitate to one of three centres of intelligence— our innate 'knowers'—the places where we know what we know:

- Head or intellectual—where thinking is domi-nant
- Heart or feeling—where emotions are dominant
- Body or gut—where instincts are dominant

These usually serve us well. However, we can over-rely on them when we're in a challenging position and become locked up. Let's break through.

2. How can I choose to be present over being perfect?

This is about imperfect people choosing to be fully present in an imperfect world, and make it better by being so.

It involves giving up chasing illusions, or being driven by perfection, long enough to be here. Right now. In an uncomfortable, messy, glorious reality.

And letting go long enough to enjoy it, because there won't be another day just like today. Ever.

The Japanese practices of *Wasi Sabi* and *Kintsugi* offer brilliant insights if you want further encouragement to shift your mindset.

3. What enables me to start where I am?

Those of us who are passionate about making a difference often want to change everything! I mean, the whole world. But making a tangible and sustainable difference is usually one step at a time.

We do need audacious ambition, but we don't have to change the world in one go. The pressure to be BIG ALL THE TIME is counterproductive. And to be a superhero is so yesterday. Subconsciously, it could also be our get-out clause, a way of hiding.

4. What can I do to face my fear?

Avoiding failure is a fool's game and takes you nowhere. And quiet disruptors are not fools...

Therefore let's lean into, rather than away from, our vulnerabilities and fears. Knowing that if we do trip up, at least we are facing the right direction. And we've moved forward, even if it's on our knees.

Face your fear and do it anyway.

5. How can I remember that 'we're all just people'?

Intellectually, we may not buy into 'we're all equal, but some are more equal than others...' But emotionally, we fall for it so often.

What are the tell-tale signs? Often it is when we are too close for comfort and find we are competing or feeling shut down.

That's when we need to face up to intimidation and re-member that 'we're all just people...' We all brush our teeth and all that stuff. We all started small. And we'll all die, eventually.

But in the meantime, we can do some great things...

Find your tone

Being heard isn't just about our words. It's also the effect of our tone. How we are encountered and experienced as thoughtful and creative change-makers.

Therefore, how we make others feel is as important as what we say. For example, are we authentic and congruent? Do we engage or just mumble from the side-lines? And are we aware of difference and can we cross boundaries?

1. Where can I practice being present?

'We can pretend to care but we can't pretend to show up'—Ashley Judd, quoted by Simon Sinek on Twitter.

As thoughtful and creative change-makers, we have the potential to make a different kind of difference. We don't have to crash around or walk over people until we force the change we want to see.

Instead, if we want to build trust and the platform for change, we have to show up. In person, bringing all that we are.

And this takes intentional practice.

2. Who are we doing this for?

Being intentional about who we are here for affects how we are experienced.

When we know *why* we are seeking change, we know *who* we are doing it for because this isn't an abstract idea. It has legs, attached to bodies.

This enables us to be clear about who we are speaking to. And also have a greater sense of what it's like to be in their shoes. It's called empathy.

3. How can I build bridges for a better world?

To bridge silos, of whatever sort, we need to be comfortable being at the boundary. However, this is difficult to do if we think our world is the only world.

Sometimes we build bridges for us to cross. And sometimes it's for others to make the journey. Either way, it requires connections across differences and letting go of assumptions about the world that we inhabit.

Being more intentional about how we look at situations and issues. But also recognising that we may be misunderstood, so watching our tone.

4. How can I cultivate more questions than answers?

Good questions are powerful. Offered with thought and generosity of spirit, they enable change rather than cause a reaction.

In posing questions, we are inviting others on the journey, rather than forcing an unchallengeable destination on them. And they are much more likely to come with us.

This is a fertile area to play with because questions are non-threatening if asked with genuine curiosity.

5. How can I know when to draw the line?

If we are seeking change, then we are starting from the belief that how things are now could be better.

However, we also need to know when enough is enough. There is a line to draw, and it's ours to own.

This aspect of developing our tone as quiet disruptors is essential. Where we draw the line and how we hold it will significantly affect how people experience us. It's not just about the words.

If our emotions dominate, we can become unhealthy, and people can't hear us. However, without them, we become less than ourselves, and our voice is weak and anaemic.

Find your rhythm

Wherever we look, there are rhythms and cycles. In nature, in life. In science and the arts. In the way people are, together, in civilisations and cultures.

Therefore why do we assume that we can just keep going like a machine? Only stopping to ask if we are efficient enough?

Uncovering our voice also means paying attention to our rhythms, the cycles that sustain us. And noticing when we're out of step.

Here are five practices that will help us find, and restore, our unique sense of rhythm. Embedding sustainable good habits in our lives so that our voice can become clearer.

1. What is a healthy way to spend my time?

'How we spend our days is, of course, how we spend our lives. What we do with this hour, and that one, is what we are doing.' So says Annie Dillard in her book *The Writing Life*

It's astonishing what we get used to and assume is normal. The current default of being 'on all the time' has its costs.

However, the answer isn't to withdraw and become a hermit. Or try and shout over the noise. Instead, we can individually rediscover a daily rhythm and environment that enables us to thrive and cultivate our voice. Because one for size does not fit all.

When and where we do our best work is an indicator. And being intentional about how to increase our creativity and curiosity all contribute to a fruitful pattern.

2. How can I build healthy seasons in my life?

Most of us are relatively cushioned from the effects of natural seasons. We live in well-built houses with controllable heating. We are used to being able to access what we want, when we want it, without waiting too long.

We have become divorced from a healthy sense of the cycles of life, and often fail to recognise when we need to embrace a seasonal shift if we are to thrive.

These seasonal triggers can be promoted by a mixture of external factors and internal responses, sometimes getting louder until we take notice.

3. How can I establish a healthy momentum?

I really appreciate the insight that 'self-discovery is a journey, not a moment'.

Journeys, like rhythm, have momentum. There is a sense of flow, which might vary over time, but doesn't stop.

Likewise uncovering our voice has momentum. The process of experimenting and learning, Of changing gear, or shifting direction over time. But it's much harder to get started or change course if we are stationary.

Sometimes we simply get stuck, especially when the obstacles seem too big. Here are some unblocking tips:

- What is the smallest thing you can do? (Dan Pink)

- What is the next right thing? (rather than trying to solve the whole)

- Why is this is the next best move? (Bernadette Jiwa)

- Write until you make sense of it (Ben Horowitz)

4. Where can I develop the rhythm of walking?

'Solvitur ambulando' it is solved by walking.

Augustine of Hippo and his 'mates' around that time (4th century) understood something profound. Movement unlocks our minds.

However, we live such sedentary lives that we've lost the habit, the rhythm, of walking. Yet it frees us up in ways that scientists are only now discovering.

Go for a walk, outdoors if possible, as it awakens our senses in a way that interiors, and air-conditioned environments, rarely do.

But don't try to resolve your issue, just enjoy the stroll. Notice what's around you. See what catches your attention. Breathe more deeply. Smile.

Even just a walk away from your desk can be beneficial. I promise.

5. What must I do to build in gaps and spaces?

Have you noticed how the gaps or spaces define what we hear as much as the notes, or words? Pauses are essential, not just to draw breath.

They give nuance and meaning, helping us interpret what we experience. For those of us developing our voice, the way we pause and cultivate life-giving habits is as important as anything else we can do.

The poet Mary Oliver's instructions for life are brilliant: 'Pay attention. Be astonished. Tell about it.'

We also need to restore our souls because the kind of voice we are talking about here isn't concerned with the repetition of information. It's the voice of a thoughtful and creative change-maker, a quiet disruptor. And it is not shallow.

Find your medium

The amazing thing about human beings is that we are so different.

How we express ourselves, how we are present, and how we inspire and influence others takes many forms.

My words might be your pictures or actions. Finding what fits us best is part of finding our voice and building a platform to use it. And it may not be what first comes to mind!

We may have been raised to value some forms of expression more highly than others. There are all sorts of layers in here, from gender and age to ethnicity and geography. The important thing is that we take time to peel off the layers that may be obscuring what our true voice sounds or looks like.

Otherwise, our voice may be lacking in resonance and clarity. And we won't be fulfilled in using it.

1. What clues are evident in your story?

Are there patterns in your story that suggest how you might best express yourself? That suggest a good fit?

For example, given their story in chapter 3, it's not at all surprising that David and Clare Hieatt are now involved with makers and mavericks.

2. Where is your home territory?

The particular expressions of quiet disruption that we covered earlier in this book are curiosity, creativity and courageous connection. It is highly likely that you found yourself naturally drawn towards one or more of these rather than equally to all three.

What is that telling you about your natural space for disruption and the medium that might work best there?

3. Where do you already have trust and attention?

What are some of the ways in which you are currently using your 'voice', even in a small measure?

Is there any evidence that you are already being heard? Where is your reputation?

And are others trusting what they hear, even if it un-settles them?

Good. Pay attention.

4. What season of work and life are you in right now?

This is a difficult but important question to ask. We need to walk in reality, infused with conviction and ambition.

This isn't a race. Nor is it a test. We need to be wise and recognise the seasons we are in. This will help shape what medium we develop.

5. Are there forms of expression you have a secret desire to try out?

Yes, do permit yourself to explore. To bring ways of expressing yourself out of the closet and try them on for size.

They may be dusty, or underdeveloped and require care and attention. But nobody is stopping you, and the likelihood is that even if this is not your significant public medium, it's useful to you as a means of exploring what you want to say and the change you are seeking to make.

Ultimately, you need to experiment. Try things out and see how they land. Talk with people who know you and believe in you. Listen to what they have to say.

Finding our voice is not a one-off activity. It takes time to grow and mature.

It also takes courage to step out and push the boundaries. To choose not to settle and risk feeling uncomfortable, and even to fail, to become the change we want to see.

19

Find your space

'Creating space'

For me, that is a delicious phrase, and has been my working refrain for as long as I can remember.

What about you?

In our overfilled world, others are unlikely to create space for you (unless they read *The Manifesto for Quiet Disruptors*).

This is your gift to yourself and your commitment to becoming the change you seek to make.

Along the way, do ask friends for help. However, the likelihood is that they will only be able to hold the door open for you. You will have to find the door and walk through it for yourself.

So how can we create space for ourselves?

Overwhelm

We all have different gauges of overwhelm. This could be emotional, physical or cognitive.

Pay attention. Be curious about what drains your energy and depletes your reserves. This isn't a judgement. It's developing your moderating capacity.

For example, for two years running, I was invited to be the MC for *BioWales*, the large annual conference for the life sciences in the Wales Millennium Centre in Cardiff. On stage, mic'd up and holding the event together.

It was an enormous privilege, and I loved it. But the first year I also spent the intervals mingling with the guests and talking with exhibitors. I was exhausted and less able to handle the real-time unpredictability that this kind of event entails.

The second year I gave myself quiet space in the intervals (including locking myself away in the bathroom). This refuelled my capacity for being present with a clear head and plenty of energy. The consequences were significant and public.

For quiet disruptors, it is likely that people, noise and pace will diminish our capacity. Accept it and create buffer zones for replenishment.

And if this isn't possible in the short term, plan for it. Otherwise, burnout is just around the corner. Believe me!

Spaciousness

This is more than just distance. For people who regularly cross boundaries, we need boundaries too.

Not boxes that confine, but zones where we can do our best work.

This may seem perverse for integrated thinkers, people who cross-fertilise. But it's about the nature of our environmental and attentional surroundings that enable us to make these connections and go deep enough in our exploration.

We need *our* space.

If our work is mainly with others, for example, in open-plan offices or team activities, we need to also build in quiet space to reflect and process. Otherwise, we drown.

I work from home—our valley and farmhouse in South West Wales—but if 'work' or clutter is visible everywhere I look, I quickly get drained.

If our days are filled with meetings, I can promise you that the work will not get done. Therefore, if you end up swallowing the line that meetings are work, take a hard look at what is really being achieved.

We need to make the scaffolding and infrastructure to create the kind of spaciousness that we need. And others may not understand.

But do it anyway. Your capacity to become the change you want to see depends on it.

Simplify

There are plenty of wise words out there from Greg McKeown, Susan Cain, Seth Godin and others who encourage us to say no. Listen to them. Take the evidence they offer to heart and strengthen your resolve.

Every time we say 'yes' to something, we are automatically saying 'no' to something else. Which may be far more significant, but we'll miss it.

The world—your world—doesn't need more 'yes' people. It has enough lemmings jumping off the cliff. But it doesn't have enough quiet disruptors, thoughtful and creative change-makers with the courage to speak softly about things that matter, and change the course of history, however local.

And you won't be able to become that change if you have too many things on your plate.

Stop. Take a hard look at what you're doing. And simplify—one small step at a time.

And the next time you are asked to do something, pause and honestly consider whether you are the best person to do this (including whether it needs doing at all). Also, face up to what it would preclude you from doing.

Is it worth it?

Sensemaking

Quiet disruptors are by nature sense-makers. Rather than taking things at face value, they are likely to probe further and ask why? And question whether this is the best way forward.

While this orientation is natural, it may be buried.

For a start, our educational system focuses on having the right answer—the one on the test sheet—rather than thinking creatively and learning more widely.

And many of our workplaces and professional training regimes are similarly structured, like a machine.

'Don't ask questions. The bosses know best...'

Except they don't, and we have a contribution to make in the emerging new world.

The good news is that we can cultivate our sensemaking.

Fundamentally, it's by finding the best space to think and reflect. To join up what may be desperate dots, find the patterns and identify dissonance.

Two very practical ways are journaling and walking. Both foster an internal rhythm that is conducive to things falling into place.

Journaling—writing, whether in a journal, on sheets of paper, or electronically—stimulates our flow of consciousness. A way of 'thinking out loud' for people who prefer quiet and who need to slow our mental wheels sufficiently to distil what is important.

The key is limiting our self-censorship and permitting ourselves to play. No one else is going to see this. It isn't the finished product. But it is a means for bringing our insights and perceptions to the surface. For working on them, rather than rushing on by.

Yes, it might be rubbish. But it least we are clearing our heads (and hearts), and there could be threads of gold that help us make more sense of what we are observing.

Walking is excellent, too.

There is something powerful in the act of movement in this way. Walking stops things churning around in our heads and frees us up to see them differently.

Just don't expect it to happen immediately. It will in its own time, including by distracting our attention and showing us a wider vista that enables our thoughts to breathe.

When I get really stuck, I walk. Even if that's just around the building.

Edge dwelling

The natural space for curious and creative change-makers is rarely in the middle of the crowd.

Even in terms of mainstream work, we are rarely in the centre. It's simply not our space, so let's get used to it.

From the edge, we can see so much more. Our perspective changes and the kinds of conversations we can have from here are profound.

But of course, it can be lonely, and we can be misunderstood. This comes with the territory, which is why we need to find fellow edge-dwellers for company.

Quiet

Ultimately, we cannot be quiet disruptors and thoughtfully creative change-makers if we do not give ourselves space to be quiet.

Obvious, yes.

But in practice, it's tough.

I can't answer this one for you. But I can encourage you to keep making the choices that will give you the opportunity for oases of stillness.

It is worth it.

You are worth it.

And the world needs who you are becoming.

So, don't give up.

20

Crossing the threshold

Globally, we are crossing a threshold.

But I didn't expect to see it so soon.

When I started writing this book, I sensed we were in the early stages of labour for a new era.

The pandemic and the dramatically raised consciousness of the impact we are having on each other and the Earth is accelerating this shift.

Birth is a messy process, and I grieve for the cost for so many people. Yet I know that we need a radically new normal because the old was broken.

And each of us, if we are going to become the change we want to see, have to cross our own thresholds.

We need to go somewhere that has not been our previous territory. Somewhere we can grow and use our voice. Where we find the courage to speak out and change the conversation.

The Answer to How is Yes.

I love this insight from Peter Block. It keeps me grounded.

It reminds me that transition is about the unknown. It is a liminal space.

I can't fully imagine what it's going to be like. And I certainly don't know how long this transition period will last.

And that's okay because I have decided to cross. And everything else will follow in time.

We can do our preparation, and we must, making sense of where we are and setting our direction. We can also build our skills and capacity, but we can never know, with 100% certainty, what is going to be like.

Instead, we can choose to step into the unknown. To use our voice, because we know conversations are needed about things that matter. Not just to us, but many others.

Because there is a world waiting for us.

And finally

I wrote this poem for fellow students at the close of *The Creative's Workshop*. It takes inspiration from the Irish philosopher poet John O'Donohue, whose work feeds my soul for the journey we are on. Enjoy.

A Blessing for the Creative Soul

Dear friends and travelling companions,
may you know
you are seen and heard,
and your work matters.
You belong.
And may you delight
in your inner being,

as the place where
your creativity flows.
Feed it well
and drink from fresh water.

May you be content to stand at the edge —
you'll see more from there.
Cherish your eyes
and follow the sightline
of your curiosity and wonder.
Protect your ears,
give them time to hear
what really matters.
The silence,
the whispers,
the roars.
And the still small voice inside.

May you choose your words and expressions
with care, because they have power
far beyond anything you can imagine.
Honour them
and offer them generously,
for they build bridges and
shape our sense of how things are.
For you are like a diamond
held up to the light.
You refract the colours around you

so that people can see what's really there.

May you grasp the vastness
of the space before you.
Enjoy your courageous imagination.
Let it take you to places
your heart longs to go.
And don't be afraid to look
your anger in the eye, knowing it's yours,
not borrowed from elsewhere.
Therefore, seek the peace of stillness,
where the clamour of other voices are muted,
and you hear your own voice with clarity.

May you embrace the mystery
of your presence,
the essence of who you are
which cannot be boxed or labelled.
Here is where your identity resides.
And may you be satisfied
as you pick up the mantle
of your unique role
in the ongoing creation of the world,
because only you can do this.

Go well — for it's time to cross this
     threshold.

Sue Heatherington, 26 June 2020

Resources

Key

W: website address
B: book title
POD: podcast title
TED: if they have a TED talk/s
On Being: if they have participated in an episode of On Being
( ): chapters where they are mentioned

ASKINOSIE Shawn
Ex lawyer, bean-to-bar chocolate maker with a justice mission
W: askinosie.com
B: *Meaningful Work*
TED
(9, 18)

BANKSY
Anonymous street artist, political activist, film director
W: walledoffhotel.com
(3, 10, 13)

BERGER Warren
Author, speaker, questionologist
W: warrenberger.com
W: amorebeautifulquestion.com
B: *A More Beautiful Question*
(5)

BLOCK Peter
Writer, community builder, consultant
W: peterblock.com
B: *The Answer to How is Yes: Acting on What Matters*
(20)

BROWN Brené
Author, research professor, speaker, courage builder
W: brenebrown.com
B: *Dare to Lead: brave work, tough conversations, whole hearts*
B: *Braving the Wilderness*
B: *Rising Strongly*
B: *Daring Greatly*
POD: Unlocking Us
TED
On Being
(3, 12, 13)

BUFFETT Warren
Investor, business magnate, philanthropist
W: berkshirehathaway.com
(7)

CAIN Susan
Author, speaker, founder of Quiet Revolution
W: quietrev.com
B: *Quiet: the power of introverts in a world that can't stop talking*
TED
(1, 3, 13, 19)

CHRISTENSEN Clayton
Business management thinker, academic
W: claytonchristensen.com
W: christenseninstitute.org
B: *The Innovator's Dilemma*
(3)

CLACHER Rachel
Artist, entrepreneur, activist, co-founder of Moneypenny
W: moneypenny.com
W: wemindthegap.org.uk
(14)

CORBETT Sarah
Gentle Protest Activist, founder of Craftivist Collective
W: craftivist-collective.com
B: *How to be a Craftivist*

TED
(10)

DOORNBOS Amos
Digital transformation strategist in humanitarian aid
W: thisisamos.com
B: *The ABCs of Responsible data*
POD: Courageous Change for Change Makers
(14)

ELIOT T S
Poet, playwright, essayist and publisher
B: *Four Quartets*
B: *The Complete Poems and Plays of T S Eliot*
(Welcome, 1)

FRIED Jason
Co-founder of Basecamp
W: basecamp.com
B: *It doesn't have to be crazy at work*
TED
(12)

GARWANDE Atul
Surgeon, writer, public health innovator
W: atulgawande.com
B: *The Checklist Manifesto*
TED
On Being
(5)

GATES Bill
Technologist, co-founder of Microsoft, philanthropist
W: gatesfoundation.org
W: gatesnotes.com
TED
(6)

GINO Francesca
Business academic, writer, speaker
W: francescagino.com
B: *Rebel Talent*

(4)

GODIN Seth
Author, entrepreneur, teacher and provocateur
W: sethgodin.com
W: seths.blog
W: akimbo.com
W: thecreativesworkshop.com
B: *Tribes*
B: *Graceful*
B: *It's Your Turn*
B: *This is Marketing*
B: *The Practice*
POD: Akimbo
TED
On Being
(1, 3, 4, 6, 17, 19)

GRANT Adam
Organisational psychologist, academic, writer, speaker
W: adamgrant.net
B: *Originals: How Nonconformists Changed the World*
B: *Give and Take*
B: *Think Again*
POD: Work Life
TED
On Being
(9)

HAMEL Gary
Business thinker, author, speaker, academic
W: garyhamel.com
B: *Humanocracy: Creating Organisations as Amazing as the People Inside Them*, with Michele Zanini
(12)

HEINEMEIER HANSSON David
Co-founder of Basecamp
W: basecamp.com
B: *It doesn't have to be crazy at work*
(12)

HERMAN Amy E
Lawyer and art historian, founder The Art of Perception
W: artfulperception.com
W: visualintelligencebook.com
B: *Visual Intelligence*
(7)

HEUGH Gideon
Poet, copywriter for TearFund
W: gideonheugh.com
B: *Devastating Beauty*
(11)

HIEATT David & Clare
Co-founders of The Hiut Denim Company and The Do
Lectures, author, speaker, encouragers
W: hiutdenim.co.uk
W: thedolectures.com
B: *Do Purpose*
B: *The Path of a Doer*
B: *Stay Curious*
(3, 17, 18)

HOLT Leslie
Mixed media artist, founder of Neuro Blooms
W: leslieholt.net
W: neuroblooms.com
(10)

HOWARTH Catherine
Activist, CEO of ShareAction
W: shareaction.org
(13)

JIWA Bernadette
Author, business storyteller and creator of the *Story Skills Workshop*
W: thestoryoftelling.com
W: therightcompany.co
W: akimbo.com/thestoryskillsworkshop
B: *Hunch*
B: *Story Driven*

B: *The Right Story*
B: *What Great Storytellers Know*
TED
(Welcome, 14, 17, 18)

JIWA Moyez
GP, medical educator, healthcare innovator, behavioural design
W: theartofdoctoring.com
W: journalofhealthdesign.com
POD: The Health Design Podcast
TED
(3, 9, 14)

KLIEN Gary
Cognitive psychologist, writer, research on insights
W: gary-klien.com
B: *Seeing what others don't*
TED
(6)

MARSHALL Steve
Writer, photographer, organisational consulting, exec development
W: drstevemarshall.com
(6)

MCKEOWN Greg
Author, speaker, social innovator
W: gregmckeown.com
B: *Essentialism: The Disciplined Pursuit of Less*
POD: What's Essential
(3, 19)

MEADE Alexa
Visual artist, 3D as 2D installations
W: alexameade.com
TED
(10)

MYCOSKIE Blake
Entrepreneur, activist, philanthropist, founder of TOMS

W: blakemycoskie.com
W: toms.com
(8)

NOVOGRATZ Jacqueline
Founder and CEO of the Acumen Fund, author
W: acumen.org
B: *Manifesto for a Moral Revolution*
TED
On Being
(14)

O'DONOHUE John
Poet, philosopher, writer
W: johnodonohue.com
B: *Benedictus: a Book of Blessings*
B: *Anam Ċara*
B: *Walking on the Pastures of Wonder*, with John Quinn
On Being
(20)

PALMER Parker
Poet, writer, teacher, activist
W: newcomerpalmer.com
On Being
(11)

PARKS Rosa
Her actions in standing up to racism, triggered the Montgomery Bus Boycott, which propelled the Civil Rights Movement in the USA in the 1950's and 1960's
(1)

REMEN Rachel Naomi
Physician, medical educator, writer
W: rachelremen.com
On Being
(6, 15)

ROBINSON Roger
Poet, writer, educator, civic citizenship
W: rogerrobinsononline.com

B: *A Portable Paradise*
On Being
(11)

ROWLAND Deborah
Organisational change consultant, writer, speaker
W: deborahrowland.com
W: still-moving.com
B: *Still Moving: How to Lead Mindful Change*
(15)

SINEK Simon
Writer, speaker, leadership expert
W: simonsinek.com
B: *Start With Why*
B: *Leaders Eat Last*
B: *The Infinite Game*
POD: A Bit of Optimism
TED
(4, 5, 13, 18)

THIMBLEBY Harold
Computer scientist, digital health, writer, academic
W: harold.thimbleby.net
B: *Fix IT: How to solve the problems of digital healthcare*
(7, 14)

THIMBLEBY Prue
Artist, storyteller, healthcare
W: pruethimbleby.net
W: artsinhealth.wales
(11)

TIPPETT Krista
Founder and CEO of The On Being Project, writer, broadcaster
W: onbeing.org
B: *Becoming Wise*
TED
On Being
(5, 14)

WHYTE David
  Poet, writer, speaker
  W: davidwhyte.com
  B: *Essentials*
  B: *Consolations: the Solace, Nourishment and Underlying Meaning of Everyday Words*
  TED
  On Being
  (11)

Resources directly connected with Quiet Disruptors
  W: quietdisruptors.com — where you will find versions of *The Manifesto for Quiet Disruptors* in a number of languages, plus other resources
  W: sueheatherington.com
  W: thewaterside.co.uk

Acknowledgements

'It takes a village to raise a child' but I also know it takes a whole community to produce a book!

And I am so grateful.

Thank you to my travelling companions from *the* Right Company, Linden Church Swansea, the first cohort of *The Creative's Workshop*, and friends from elsewhere. You are a part of me in ways I could not have previously imagined.

In particular I have appreciated the practical support and cheering on from Katia Lord, Alison Coates, Lina Yang, Brandon Berry, James Geier, Jennifer Hole, Ruth Dent, Amos Doornbos, Tracy Ingham, Harold Thimbleby, Bernadette Jiwa, Chris Matthews, Arlette Manasseh, Alastair Duncan, Em Boucher, Mo Baldwin, Alan and Wanda Woodward, Alison Jones, Brian Peltier, Jan Russell and Lyn King. And special thanks to Jim and Wendy McConnell who started sending me the cost of a packet of pencils to encourage me to keep on writing—over two years ago.

None of this would have happened without my life companion and best friend, Steve. Without his technical wizardry this book simply would not have seen the light of day.

Diolch yn fawr iawn i bawb—that's Welsh for thanks very much everyone

About the Author

Sue Heatherington has walked a different path for as long as she can remember. Often ahead of her time, noticing what's emerging, and encouraging those who are working at the edge.

Her background is unusually broad, reflecting her ease at crossing boundaries, from rural development research, through planning, marketing and business management to a decade as a pioneering chief executive in the UK National Health Service.

Leaving the NHS in 2009, Sue trained as a professional coach and worked as a consultant and facilitator with senior teams and emerging leaders across a range of industries. She is now a writer, catalyst and thinking partner for people and teams creating change that matters.

Originally from a farm in Kent, England, Sue and her husband Steve run The Waterside, a 40-acre valley in South West Wales. It is also home to Jules, Sue's learning disabled brother, and their herd of alpacas.